CHRISTMAS HITS
FOR TWO

ISBN 978-1-4950-6919-2

HAL•LEONARD®
CORPORATION
7777 W. BLUEMOUND RD. P.O. BOX 13819 MILWAUKEE, WI 53213

For all works contained herein:
Unauthorized copying, arranging, adapting, recording, Internet posting, public performance,
or other distribution of the printed music in this publication is an infringement of copyright.
Infringers are liable under the law.

Visit Hal Leonard Online at
www.halleonard.com

CONTENTS

ALL I WANT FOR CHRISTMAS IS YOU

ALTO SAXES

Words and Music by MARIAH CAREY
and WALTER AFANASIEFF

Copyright © 1994 BEYONDIDOLIZATION, SONY/ATV MUSIC PUBLISHING LLC, TAMAL VISTA MUSIC,
WALLYWORLD MUSIC and KOBALT MUSIC COPYRIGHTS SARL
All Rights for BEYONDIDOLIZATION Controlled and Administered by UNIVERSAL TUNES, A Division of SONGS OF UNIVERSAL, INC.
All Rights for SONY/ATV MUSIC PUBLISHING LLC, TAMAL VISTA MUSIC and WALLYWORLD MUSIC Administered by
SONY/ATV MUSIC PUBLISHING LLC, 424 Church Street, Suite 1200, Nashville, TN 37219
All Rights Reserved   Used by Permission

BABY, IT'S COLD OUTSIDE
from the Motion Picture NEPTUNE'S DAUGHTER

ALTO SAXES

By FRANK LOESSER

© 1948 (Renewed) FRANK MUSIC CORP.
All Rights Reserved

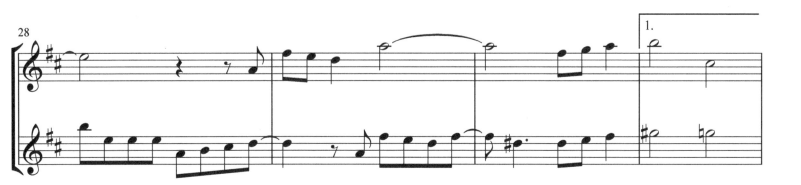

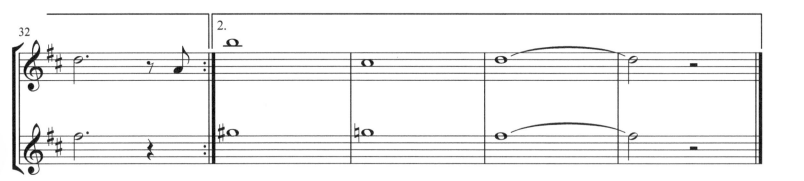

THE CHRISTMAS SONG
(Chestnuts Roasting on an Open Fire)

ALTO SAXES

Music and Lyric by MEL TORMÉ
and ROBERT WELLS

Moderately slow

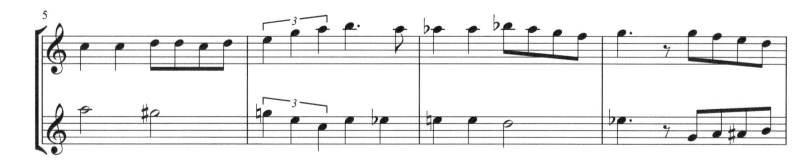

© 1946 (Renewed) EDWIN H. MORRIS & COMPANY, A Division of MPL Music Publishing, Inc. and SONY/ATV MUSIC PUBLISHING LLC
All Rights on behalf of SONY/ATV MUSIC PUBLISHING LLC Administered by
SONY/ATV MUSIC PUBLISHING LLC, 424 Church Street, Suite 1200, Nashville, TN 37219
All Rights Reserved

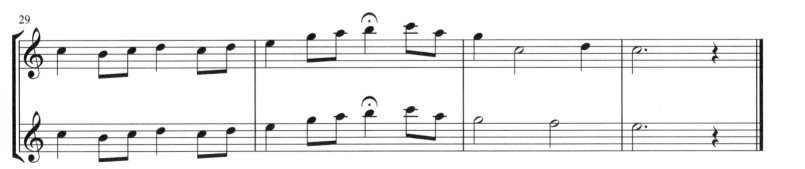

THE CHRISTMAS WALTZ

ALTO SAXES

Words by SAMMY CAHN
Music by JULE STYNE

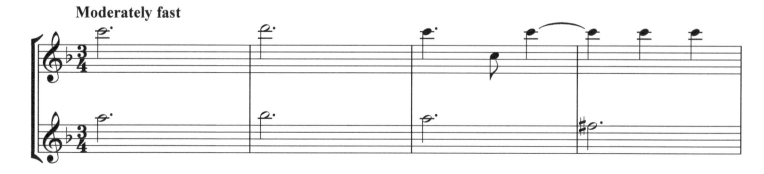

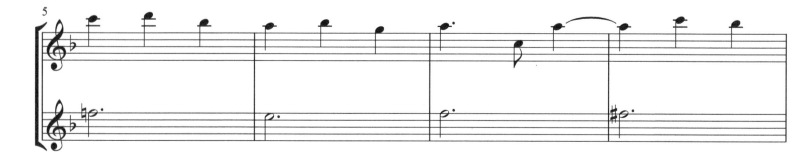

© 1954 (Renewed) PRODUCERS MUSIC PUBLISHING CO., INC. and CAHN MUSIC CO.
All Rights for PRODUCERS MUSIC PUBLISHING CO., INC. Administered by CHAPPELL & CO., INC.
All Rights for CAHN MUSIC CO. Administered by IMAGEM SOUNDS
All Rights Reserved   Used by Permission

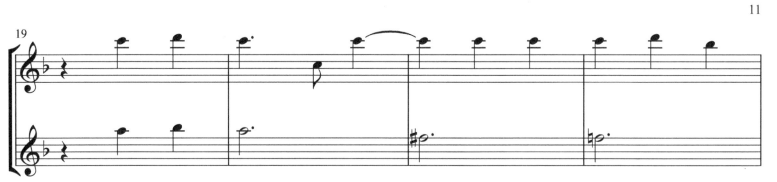

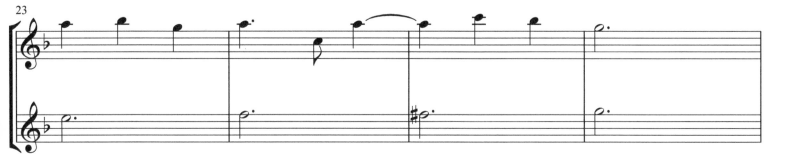

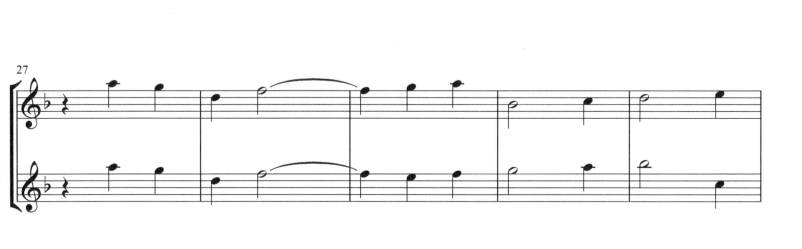

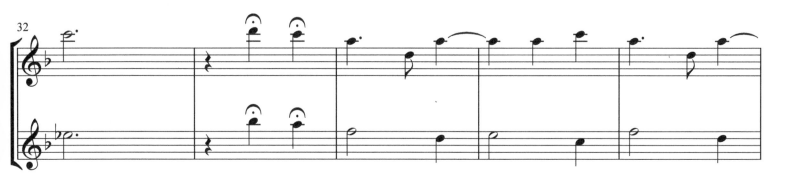

DO YOU HEAR WHAT I HEAR

ALTO SAXES

Words and Music by NOEL REGNEY
and GLORIA SHAYNE

Moderately

Copyright © 1962 (Renewed) by Jewel Music Publishing Co., Inc. (ASCAP)
International Copyright Secured   All Rights Reserved
Used by Permission

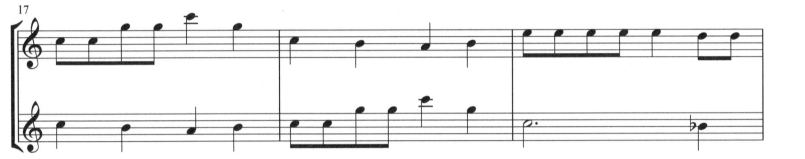

DO YOU WANT TO BUILD A SNOWMAN?

from FROZEN

ALTO SAXES

Music and Lyrics by KRISTEN ANDERSON-LOPEZ
and ROBERT LOPEZ

Moderately fast

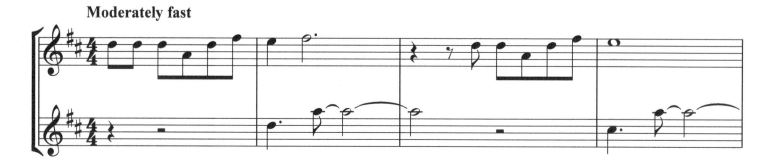

© 2013 Wonderland Music Company, Inc.
All Rights Reserved. Used by Permission.

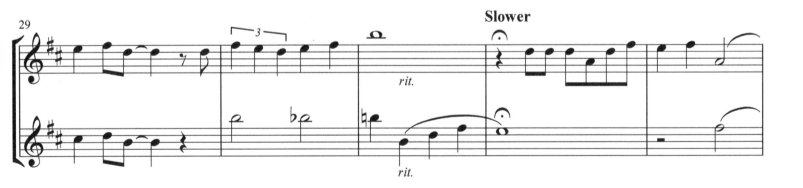

FELIZ NAVIDAD

ALTO SAXES

Music and Lyrics by
JOSÉ FELICIANO

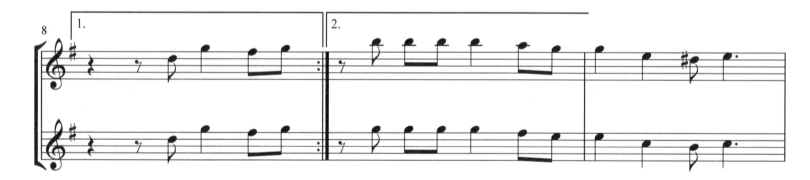

Copyright © 1970 J & H Publishing Company (ASCAP)
Copyright Renewed
All Rights Administered by Law, P.A. o/b/o J & H Publishing Company
International Copyright Secured   All Rights Reserved

HAVE YOURSELF A MERRY LITTLE CHRISTMAS

from MEET ME IN ST. LOUIS

ALTO SAXES

Words and Music by HUGH MARTIN
and RALPH BLANE

Moderately slow

© 1943 (Renewed) METRO-GOLDWYN-MAYER INC.
© 1944 (Renewed) EMI FEIST CATALOG INC.
All Rights Controlled and Administered by EMI FEIST CATALOG INC. (Publishing) and ALFRED MUSIC (Print)
All Rights Reserved   Used by Permission

HERE COMES SANTA CLAUS
(Right Down Santa Claus Lane)

ALTO SAXES

Words and Music by GENE AUTRY
and OAKLEY HALDEMAN

© 1947 (Renewed) Gene Autry's Western Music Publishing Co.
All Rights Reserved   Used by Permission

A HOLLY JOLLY CHRISTMAS

ALTO SAXES

Music and Lyrics by
JOHNNY MARKS

Moderately bright

Copyright © 1962, 1964 (Renewed 1990, 1992) St. Nicholas Music Inc., 254 W. 54th Street, 12th Floor, New York, New York 10019
All Rights Reserved

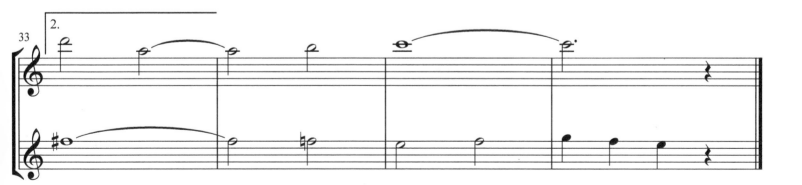

(There's No Place Like)

HOME FOR THE HOLIDAYS

ALTO SAXES

Words and Music by AL STILLMAN
and ROBERT ALLEN

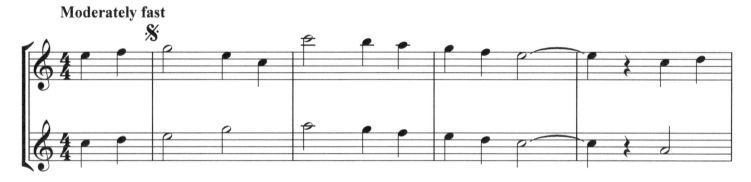

© Copyright 1954 (Renewed) by Music Sales Corporation (ASCAP) and Charlie Deitcher Productions
International Copyright Secured   All Rights Reserved   Used by Permission

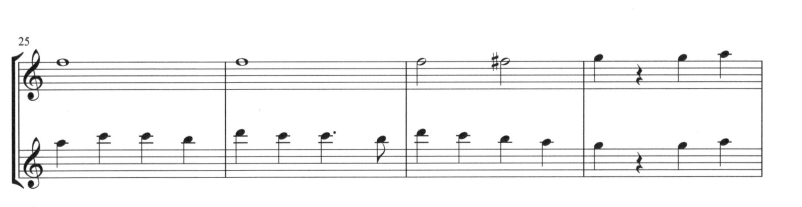

D.S. al Fine

I'LL BE HOME FOR CHRISTMAS

ALTO SAXES

Words and Music by KIM GANNON
and WALTER KENT

Moderately

© Copyright 1943 by Gannon & Kent Music Co., Inc., Beverly Hills, CA
Copyright Renewed
International Copyright Secured   All Rights Reserved

IT'S BEGINNING TO LOOK LIKE CHRISTMAS

ALTO SAXES

By MEREDITH WILLSON

Moderately bright

© 1951 PLYMOUTH MUSIC CO., INC.
© Renewed 1979 FRANK MUSIC CORP. and MEREDITH WILLSON MUSIC
All Rights Reserved

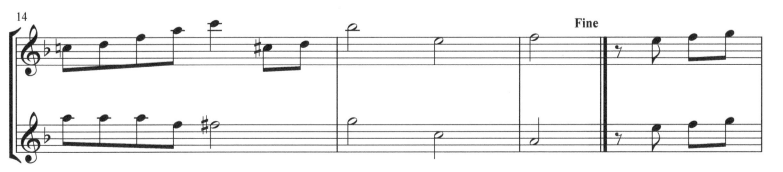

LET IT SNOW! LET IT SNOW! LET IT SNOW!

ALTO SAXES

Words by SAMMY CAHN
Music by JULE STYNE

© 1945 (Renewed) PRODUCERS MUSIC PUBLISHING CO., INC. and CAHN MUSIC CO.
All Rights for PRODUCERS MUSIC PUBLISHING CO., INC. Administered by CHAPPELL & CO., INC.
All Rights for CAHN MUSIC CO. Administered by IMAGEM SOUNDS
All Rights Reserved   Used by Permission

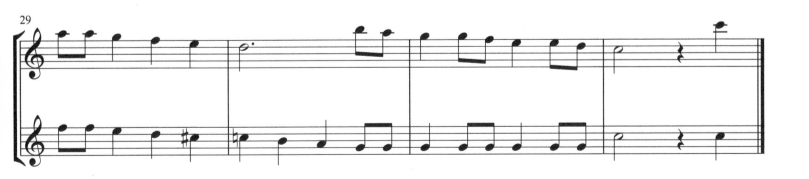

MARY, DID YOU KNOW?

ALTO SAXES

Words and Music by MARK LOWRY
and BUDDY GREENE

© 1991 Word Music, LLC and Rufus Music (administered at CapitolCMGPublishing.com)
All Rights Reserved   Used by Permission

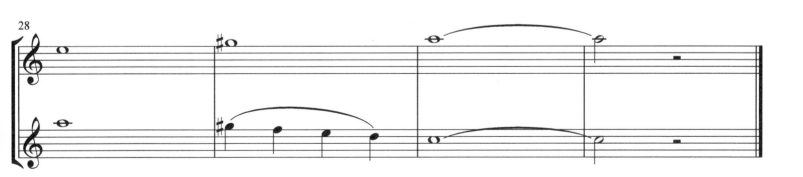

THE MOST WONDERFUL TIME OF THE YEAR

ALTO SAXES

Words and Music by EDDIE POLA
and GEORGE WYLE

Moderately, in 1

Copyright © 1963 Barnaby Music Corp.
Copyright Renewed
Administered by Lichelle Music Company
International Copyright Secured   All Rights Reserved

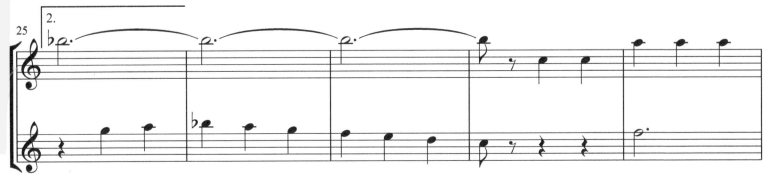

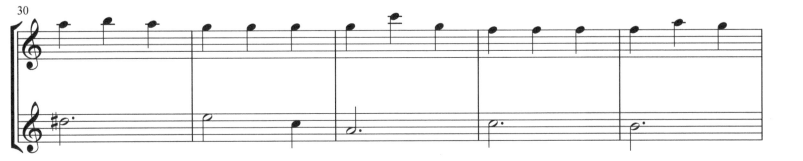

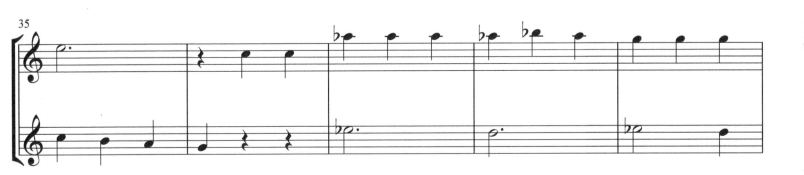

D.S. al Coda
(no repeat)

CODA

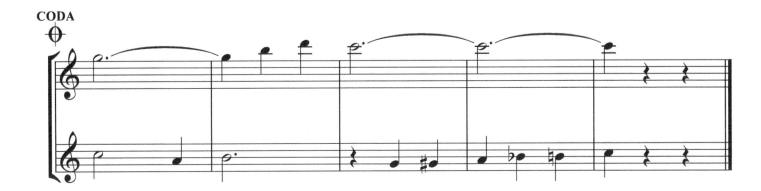

MY FAVORITE THINGS
from THE SOUND OF MUSIC

ALTO SAXES

Lyrics by OSCAR HAMMERSTEIN II
Music by RICHARD RODGERS

Copyright © 1959 by Richard Rodgers and Oscar Hammerstein II
Copyright Renewed
Williamson Music, a Division of Rodgers & Hammerstein: an Imagem Company, owner of publication and allied rights throughout the world
International Copyright Secured   All Rights Reserved

ROCKIN' AROUND THE CHRISTMAS TREE

ALTO SAXES

Music and Lyrics by
JOHNNY MARKS

Copyright © 1958 (Renewed 1986) St. Nicholas Music Inc., 254 W. 54th Street, 12th Floor, New York, New York 10019
All Rights Reserved

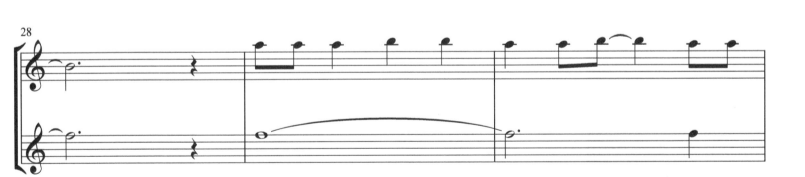

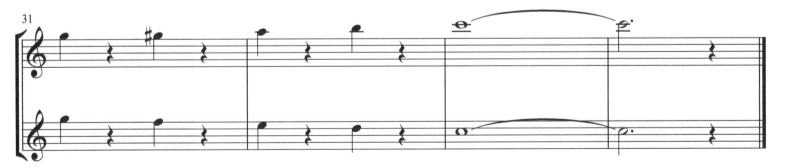

RUDOLPH THE RED-NOSED REINDEER

ALTO SAXES

Music and Lyrics by
JOHNNY MARKS

Copyright © 1949 (Renewed 1977) St. Nicholas Music Inc., 254 W. 54th Street, 12th Floor, New York, New York 10019
All Rights Reserved

SILVER BELLS
from the Paramount Picture THE LEMON DROP KID

ALTO SAXES

Words and Music by JAY LIVINGSTON
and RAY EVANS

Moderately

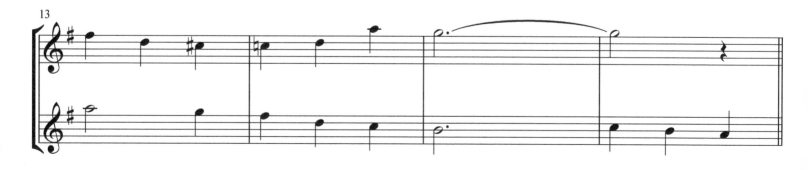

Copyright © 1950 Sony/ATV Music Publishing LLC
Copyright Renewed
All Rights Administered by Sony/ATV Music Publishing LLC, 424 Church Street, Suite 1200, Nashville, TN 37219
International Copyright Secured   All Rights Reserved

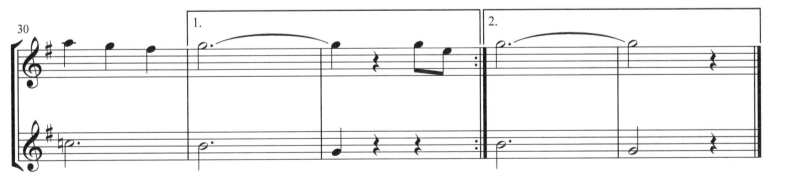

SOMEWHERE IN MY MEMORY

from the Twentieth Century Fox Motion Picture HOME ALONE

ALTO SAXES

Words by LESLIE BRICUSSE
Music by JOHN WILLIAMS

Moderately

Copyright © 1990 Fox Film Music Corporation and John Hughes Songs
All Rights for John Hughes Songs Administered by Warner-Tamerlane Publishing Corp.
All Rights Reserved Used by Permission

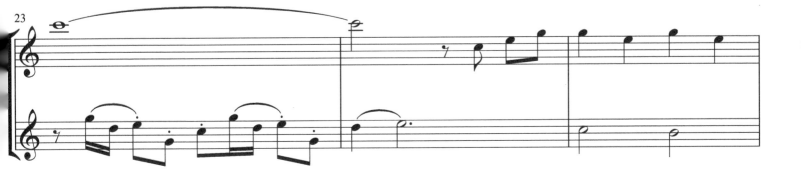

WHITE CHRISTMAS
from the Motion Picture Irving Berlin's HOLIDAY INN

ALTO SAXES

Words and Music by
IRVING BERLIN

© Copyright 1940, 1942 by Irving Berlin
Copyright Renewed
International Copyright Secured   All Rights Reserved

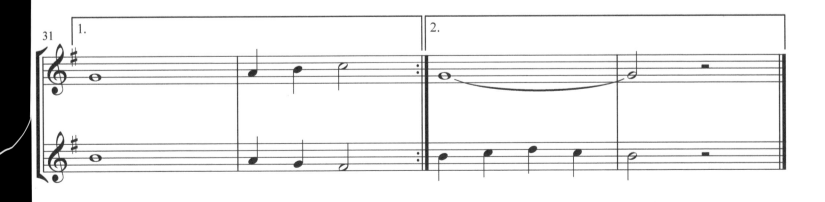

HAL•LEONARD INSTRUMENTAL PLAY-ALONG

Your favorite songs are arranged just for solo instrumentalists with this outstanding series. Each book includes great full-accompaniment play-along audio so you can sound just like a pro!

Check out **halleonard.com** for songlists, more titles, or to order online from your favorite music retailer.

12 Pop Hits
12 songs • $14.99 each
00261790	Flute	00261795	Horn
00261791	Clarinet	00261796	Trombone
00261792	Alto Sax	00261797	Violin
00261793	Tenor Sax	00261798	Viola
00261794	Trumpet	00261799	Cello

The Very Best of Bach
15 selections • $12.99 each
00225371	Flute	00225376	Horn
00225372	Clarinet	00225377	Trombone
00225373	Alto Sax	00225378	Violin
00225374	Tenor Sax	00225379	Viola
00225375	Trumpet	00225380	Cello

The Beatles
15 songs • $14.99 each
00225330	Flute	00225335	Horn
00225331	Clarinet	00225336	Trombone
00225332	Alto Sax	00225337	Violin
00225333	Tenor Sax	00225338	Viola
00225334	Trumpet	00225339	Cello

Chart Hits
12 songs • $14.99 each
00146207	Flute	00146212	Horn
00146208	Clarinet	00146213	Trombone
00146209	Alto Sax	00146214	Violin
00146210	Tenor Sax	00146215	Viola
00146211	Trumpet	00146216	Cello

Christmas Songs
12 songs • $12.99 each
00146855	Flute	00146863	Horn
00146858	Clarinet	00146864	Trombone
00146859	Alto Sax	00146866	Violin
00146860	Tenor Sax	00146867	Viola
00146862	Trumpet	00146868	Cello

Contemporary Broadway
15 songs • $14.99 each
00298704	Flute	00298709	Horn
00298705	Clarinet	00298710	Trombone
00298706	Alto Sax	00298711	Violin
00298707	Tenor Sax	00298712	Viola
00298708	Trumpet	00298713	Cello

Disney Movie Hits
12 songs • $14.99 each
00841420	Flute	00841424	Horn
00841687	Oboe	00841425	Trombone
00841421	Clarinet	00841426	Violin
00841422	Alto Sax	00841427	Viola
00841686	Tenor Sax	00841428	Cello
00841423	Trumpet		

Prices, contents, and availability subject to change without notice.

Disney characters and artwork ™ & © 2021 Disney

Disney Solos
12 songs • $14.99 each
00841404	Flute	00841506	Oboe
00841406	Alto Sax	0841409	Trumpet
00841407	Horn	00841410	Violin
00841411	Viola	00841412	Cello
00841405	Clarinet/Tenor Sax		
00841408	Trombone/Baritone		
00841553	Mallet Percussion		

Dixieland Favorites
15 songs • $12.99 each
00268756	Flute	0068759	Trumpet
00268757	Clarinet	00268760	Trombone
00268758	Alto Sax		

Billie Eilish
9 songs • $14.99 each
00345648	Flute	00345653	Horn
00345649	Clarinet	00345654	Trombone
00345650	Alto Sax	00345655	Violin
00345651	Tenor Sax	00345656	Viola
00345652	Trumpet	00345657	Cello

Favorite Movie Themes
13 songs • $14.99 each
00841166	Flute	00841168	Trumpet
00841167	Clarinet	00841170	Trombone
00841169	Alto Sax	00841296	Violin

Gospel Hymns
15 songs • $12.99 each
00194648	Flute	00194654	Trombone
00194649	Clarinet	00194655	Violin
00194650	Alto Sax	00194656	Viola
00194651	Tenor Sax	00194657	Cello
00194652	Trumpet		

Great Classical Themes
15 songs • $12.99 each
00292727	Flute	00292733	Horn
00292728	Clarinet	00292735	Trombone
00292729	Alto Sax	00292736	Violin
00292730	Tenor Sax	00292737	Viola
00292732	Trumpet	00292738	Cello

The Greatest Showman
8 songs • $14.99 each
00277389	Flute	00277394	Horn
00277390	Clarinet	00277395	Trombone
00277391	Alto Sax	00277396	Violin
00277392	Tenor Sax	00277397	Viola
00277393	Trumpet	00277398	Cello

Irish Favorites
31 songs • $12.99 each
00842489	Flute	00842495	Trombone
00842490	Clarinet	00842496	Violin
00842491	Alto Sax	00842497	Viola
00842493	Trumpet	00842498	Cello
00842494	Horn		

Michael Jackson
11 songs • $14.99 each
00119495	Flute	00119499	Trumpet
00119496	Clarinet	00119501	Trombone
00119497	Alto Sax	00119503	Violin
00119498	Tenor Sax	00119502	Accomp.

Jazz & Blues
14 songs • $14.99 each
00841438	Flute	00841441	Trumpet
00841439	Clarinet	00841443	Trombone
00841440	Alto Sax	00841444	Violin
00841442	Tenor Sax		

Jazz Classics
12 songs • $12.99 each
00151812	Flute	00151816	Trumpet
00151813	Clarinet	00151818	Trombone
00151814	Alto Sax	00151819	Violin
00151815	Tenor Sax	00151821	Cello

Les Misérables
13 songs • $14.99 each
00842292	Flute	00842297	Horn
00842293	Clarinet	00842298	Trombone
00842294	Alto Sax	00842299	Violin
00842295	Tenor Sax	00842300	Viola
00842296	Trumpet	00842301	Cello

Metallica
12 songs • $14.99 each
02501327	Flute	02502454	Horn
02501339	Clarinet	02501329	Trombone
02501332	Alto Sax	02501334	Violin
02501333	Tenor Sax	02501335	Viola
02501330	Trumpet	02501338	Cello

Motown Classics
15 songs • $12.99 each
00842572	Flute	00842576	Trumpet
00842573	Clarinet	00842578	Trombone
00842574	Alto Sax	00842579	Violin
00842575	Tenor Sax		

Pirates of the Caribbean
16 songs • $14.99 each
00842183	Flute	00842188	Horn
00842184	Clarinet	00842189	Trombone
00842185	Alto Sax	00842190	Violin
00842186	Tenor Sax	00842191	Viola
00842187	Trumpet	00842192	Cello

Queen
17 songs • $14.99 each
00285402	Flute	00285407	Horn
00285403	Clarinet	00285408	Trombone
00285404	Alto Sax	00285409	Violin
00285405	Tenor Sax	00285410	Viola
00285406	Trumpet	00285411	Cello

Simple Songs
14 songs • $12.99 each
00249081	Flute	00249087	Horn
00249092	Oboe	00249089	Trombone
00249082	Clarinet	00249090	Violin
00249083	Alto Sax	00249091	Viola
00249084	Tenor Sax	00249092	Cello
00249086	Trumpet	00249094	Mallets

Superhero Themes
14 songs • $14.99 each
00363195	Flute	00363200	Horn
00363196	Clarinet	00363201	Trombone
00363197	Alto Sax	00363202	Violin
00363198	Tenor Sax	00363203	Viola
00363199	Trumpet	00363204	Cello

Star Wars
16 songs • $16.99 each
00350900	Flute	00350907	Horn
00350913	Oboe	00350908	Trombone
00350903	Clarinet	00330909	Violin
00350904	Alto Sax	00350910	Viola
00350905	Tenor Sax	00350911	Cello
00350906	Trumpet	00350914	Mallet

Taylor Swift
15 songs • $12.99 each
00842532	Flute	00842537	Horn
00842533	Clarinet	00842538	Trombone
00842534	Alto Sax	00842539	Violin
00842535	Tenor Sax	00842540	Viola
00842536	Trumpet	00842541	Cello

Video Game Music
13 songs • $12.99 each
00283877	Flute	00283883	Horn
00283878	Clarinet	00283884	Trombone
00283879	Alto Sax	00283885	Violin
00283880	Tenor Sax	00283886	Viola
00283882	Trumpet	00283887	Cello

Wicked
13 songs • $12.99 each
00842236	Flute	00842241	Horn
00842237	Clarinet	00842242	Trombone
00842238	Alto Sax	00842243	Violin
00842239	Tenor Sax	00842244	Viola
00842240	Trumpet	00842245	Cello

HAL•LEONARD®